LAYO IS A V*RGIN WHO CAN'T DRIVE

Laya needs to work on those dance moves
Quite a yikes

Bella needs to stop
this Elena rubbish!

layo & belle are fugly
snakes! do **NOT** trust them

BELLA IS A WH*RE WHO CAN'T DRIVE

PHAT ASS SAZ HAS A PHAT ASS PREGGO BELLY

CHI IS A F*CKING CLOWN. DIDN'T EVEN REALISE HE WAS WEARING A COSTUME...

LAYO HAS A TINY CHODE

TARE BAITLY WANTED AN EXCUSE TO GET HER TITS OUT!

IS THIS LAYO'S COMING OUT PARTY?

30/10/22

LAYO
X
DWIGHT

BELLA
X
ELENA

HORNY 4
DWIGHT !

→ THREESOME
WITH ELENA?

XOXO

Layo really
Party Rock Anthem!

#wattpad
#halloween
#badbitches
#paddington

Layo and Bella need
therapy !!

stoncini is a big __ass__ sicko.
someone needs to sensor
her full time.

Printed in Great Britain
by Amazon

87094333R00072